Online Legal Research

A Guide to Accompany

2006-2007
Business Law and Legal Environment Texts by

Roger LeRoy Miller
Gaylord A. Jentz
Frank B. Cross

Guide prepared by

Roger LeRoy Miller
Institute for University Studies
Arlington, Texas

William Eric Hollowell
Member of
   U. S. Supreme Court Bar
   Minnesota State Bar
   Florida State Bar

THOMSON
✴ ™
SOUTH-WESTERN
WEST

Australia · Canada · Mexico · Singapore · Spain · United Kingdom · United States

Online Legal Research Guide, 2006-2007 Edition
A Guide to Accompany 2006-2007 Business Law and Legal Environment Texts by Roger LeRoy Miller, Gaylord A. Jentz, and Frank B. Cross

Vice President/Editorial Director:
Jack Calhoun

Publisher for Business Law & Accounting:
Rob Dewey

Acquisitions Editor:
Steven Silverstein

Senior Developmental Editor:
Jan Lamar

Executive Marketing Manager:
Lisa Lysne

Production Editors:
Bill Stryker and Ann Sheroff

Manufacturing Coordinator:
Charlene Taylor

Printer:
West Printing Company

Preface

As you will discover when you read the 2006 and 2007 editions of the business law and legal environment texts written by Roger LeRoy Miller, Gaylord A. Jentz, and Frank B. Cross, the law changes relatively slowly. The same used to be said about how to find the law, or, otherwise stated, about how to do legal research. Today, nothing could be further from the truth, for those looking for information about business law and the legal environment of business have a whole new world of research resources, literally at their fingertips. The amount of new resources coming online is changing every day and so, too, is the speed at which such legal resources can be accessed.

In this booklet that we have prepared to accompany all of the 2006 and 2007 editions of the texts by Roger LeRoy Miller, Gaylord Jentz, and Frank B. Cross, we provide you with much basic information about how to find almost anything related to law on the Internet. As you read in your text, you noted that whenever possible, we provide a Web address for court cases. In addition, there are many other aspects of the law that you can research on the Internet. We hope that this book will help you feel comfortable moving around the Web as you seek out useful legal information.

Remember that you should always be accessing the specific Web site for your text, which is given in the preface of each text written by Roger LeRoy Miller, Gaylord A. Jentz, and Frank B. Cross. This book-specific Web site address can also be found at the very end of every chapter in your business law and legal environment text.

There you will find online quizzes for each chapter in your text. You will also find Internet exercises that are referred to at the end of each chapter in your text. Finally, you can easily link to our *general* business law and legal environment Web site (**www.westbuslaw.com**) at which you will find new cases for each business law and legal environment subject, as well as numerous other helpful data for your studies in business law and the legal environment. In addition, you can access digital videos at the book-specific web site.

We end this preface with a warning: Things change quickly on the Web! As of the printing of this booklet, all Web addresses were working.

R. L. M.
E. W. H.

TABLE OF CONTENTS

Page

INTRODUCTION

In this booklet to accompany all of the 2006 and 2007 editions of the business law and legal environment texts written by Roger LeRoy Miller, Gaylord A. Jentz, and Frank B. Cross, we will tell you how to think like an online researcher, how to do online research better and faster, and take you to some of the best resources currently available on the Internet. We will also define and discuss browsers, search engines, and other terms that relate to aspects of engaging in research online.

By the time you read this booklet, some of what we say will have changed—the resources on the Internet will have improved, some resources will have been removed, and some will have been added. The general approach to conducting research online will not have changed, however. The first steps will always be to know the object of your research, to determine whether the Internet is the right tool for your project, and to narrow the focus of your search to find exactly the information that you need. If you can master these steps, you will be able to conduct research on the Internet no matter how much it changes.

INTERNET TOOLS

User-friendly software, color monitors and printers, and faster processors have combined with other technological advances to open the Internet to anyone with only modest computer knowledge. With a few points and clicks, you can get onto, and maneuver around the Internet.

UNIFORM RESOURCE LOCATORS
A uniform resource locator (URL) is an Internet "address." You might think of a URL as an electronic citation. A URL identifies nearly every resource on the Internet.

The basic format of a URL is "service://directorypath/filename." For example, __http://www.westbuslaw.com__ is the URL for the West Legal Resources Web site, a resource center for business law and legal environment instructors and students using West Legal Studies in Business college textbooks. This particular URL indicates that you will be using the "http" service to reach the directory path **http://www.westbuslaw.com.** This site provides access to instructor resources, new textbook and learning material releases, and an online catalog and bookstore.

"http" is an abbreviation for **hypertext transfer protocol**. When something on the Internet is a site on the World Wide Web, the first part of its address is "http." Hypertext is a database system within which disparate objects (text, graphics, and so on) can be linked to each other. With hypertext, you can move from one object to another even though their forms are different (for example, text and graphics have different forms). Protocol is the system of formats and rules that enable two computers to communicate. (*Because "http://" is part of the URL of every site on the Web, we have normally omitted it from the rest of the URLs included in this booklet.* In your text, in contrast, we include them, because certain URLs require the http:// before the rest of the address.)

"www" is an abbreviation for World Wide Web. The **World Wide Web**, or simply the Web, is a hypertext-based service through which data are made available on the Internet.

To enter a URL into a browser, you often do not need to type in http and www. The browser will enter these terms automatically. This saves time.

WORLD WIDE WEB

The World Wide Web (the Web) is a data service on the Internet. The Web is accessed through a browser. The browser's basic user interface is *hypertext*, which means that communications between computers on the Web are primarily through links and menus (lists of commands).

When most people think of the Internet, they think of the Web. The Web consists primarily of documents, which are referred to as Web pages (sometimes **home pages**) or Web sites. These pages or sites usually contain links (sometimes called hot links) in boldface, underlined, or colored text. By selecting or clicking on an electronic link, a user can be transported to other pages or sites, or run other software. From the Web, text, graphics, and software can be downloaded (or selected portions can be cut and pasted into a word processing document on your computer).

For example, the Legal Information Institute at Cornell Law School has one of the best law-related sites on the Internet (see **www.law.cornell.edu/**). By clicking on the links within that Web site, you can find, for instance, the U.S. Constitution, the U.S. Code, or selected court cases, including the most recent United States Supreme Court decisions, as well as some of the Court's historic decisions.

LEGAL RESEARCH

Legal research includes a search for material that indicates how a judge will resolve a certain issue. This is because, in our legal system, judges interpret what the law is and how it is applied.

Traditionally, legal research involved using the material available in a law library or conducting a search through a commercial, fee-based computerized database such as Westlaw®. With the Internet, a third option has emerged. You can undertake much legal research online often at no charge.

What can be found on the Internet includes the following *primary sources* of law.

- The United States Constitution, U.S. treaties, the Declaration of Independence, and other selected important historical documents.
- United States Supreme Court decisions.
- Decisions issued by the U.S. Courts of Appeals over at least the last two or three years.
- The entire U.S. Code (all federal statutes). See the U.S. House of Representatives Office of the Law Revision Counsel at **http://uscode.house.gov/**.
- The entire Code of Federal Regulations (all federal administrative agency rules). For example, the National Archives and Records Administration at **www.gpoaccess.gov/cfr/index.html** includes the Code of Federal Regulations.
- Materials focused on specific areas of the law such as intellectual property.
- Sources related to each state's law vary in the depth of their coverage. There is a list of numerous and varied state resources indexed at: **www.llsdc.org/sourcebook/state-leg.htm**.
- Foreign law, which can be hard to find in many law libraries, can be found at such sites as the European Union Internet Resources site at **www.lib.berkeley.edu/GSSI/eu.html**.

What is available online in terms of secondary sources of law (comments or explanations by experts on particular topics) also varies. Traditional secondary sources, such as the legal encyclopedias and legal treatises familiar to paralegals and lawyers in their print versions, are generally *not* available. Other sources are online, however, to help a researcher focus his or her research (see, for example, the resources provided by Nolo Press at **www.nolo.com/**). In addition, many law firms provide background material at their sites.

FACT-BASED RESEARCH
The Internet is very good for peripheral research of all kinds. The great value of the Internet to all researchers is in the wealth of nonlegal information available. This includes, among other things, library catalogs, phone books, public records, company Web sites, and databases of nonlegal government information. For example, some government agencies plan to put all of their files online, making them instantly available to anyone who needs the information that they contain. (An excellent starting point for federal agency information is the Government Information Locator Service at **www.access.gpo.gov/su docs/gils/index.html** .)

ACCESSING AND NAVIGATING THE INTERNET

The Internet can be compared to an enormous library. Knowing how to get into the library—how to gain access to the information you need—is one of most important parts of any research, and this is true of using the Internet. To get into a library, you need to know where it is and you need to go through the door. To get onto the Internet, you also need to find it and to go there—with a computer and an online service or an Internet service provider.

Once you have access to the information, the next important step is to find your way through the vast number of resources to the right information. In a library, this is done with the help of a card catalog (or the library's computerized catalog). On the Internet, this is done with the help of browsers, guides, directories, and search engines.

NAVIGATING THE INTERNET

As stated earlier, the Internet is similar to an enormous library, but there is a key difference—the Internet has no centralized, comprehensive card catalog. In place of a card catalog, a researcher uses browsers (usually Microsoft's Internet Explorer), guides, directories, and search engines.

GUIDES AND DIRECTORIES
The lack of a single, comprehensive catalog to what is available on the Internet has led to hundreds of attempts to survey and map the Web. Lists of Web sites categorized by subject are organized into guides and directories, which can be accessed at Web sites online. These sites provide menus of topics that are

usually subdivided into narrower subtopics, which themselves may be subdivided, until a list of URLs is reached. If you are uncertain of which menu to use, directories allow you to run a search of the directory site. Popular examples of online directories include Yahoo! (**www.yahoo.com**) and, for legal researchers, FindLaw (**www.findlaw.com**). FindLaw, now part of West Group, offers an increasingly complete array of resources. Here are some of the topic areas in the law: Cases & Codes; US Federal Resources; Forms; Legal Subjects; Software & Technology; Reference Resources; Law Student Resources; and many others. You should familiarize yourself with FindLaw before you undertake any legal research.

SEARCH ENGINES

Next to browsers, the most important tools for conducting research on the Web are the search engines. Search engines include:

- Google (**www.google.com**)
- Vivisimo (**http://vivisimo.com/**)
- AltaVista (**www.altavista.com**)
- MSN Search (**http://search.msn.com**)
- AOL Search (**http://search.aol.com**)
- Excite (**www.excite.com**)
- Lycos (**www.hotbot.com/**)
- AskJeeves (**www.ask.com**)

A search engine scans the Web and indexes the contents of pages into a database. In contrast with directories, which people normally compile, a computer generates most of the results with a search engine. This means that the limits on those results are the researcher's ability to phrase a query within the constraints of the search engine's capabilities.

Another search engine is Teoma (**www.teoma.com**). Some people like its "Refine" feature, which offers suggested topics to explore after you do a search. The "Resources" section of results is also unique, pointing users to pages that specifically serve as link resources about various topics.

There are search engines that will search only specific categories of resources, particularly for law research. For example, FindLaw provides a tool at **http://lawcrawler.findlaw.com/** that searches only legal resources on the Web. This FindLaw tool can be further limited to search specified databases such as federal government sites only.

Search engines vary in the size and scope of searches, in the flexibility of possible queries, and in the presentation of results. For legal research, however, even the best search engine cannot match the results of a search conducted with the internal search engine of a commercial fee-based database such as Lexis® (**www.lexis.com**) or Westlaw® (**www.westlaw.com**). For example, all search engines have the capability to use connectors, such as "and," "or," and "not." For most search engines, this is the limit of their sophistication. More precise queries can be formulated with Westlaw®, especially for a researcher proficient in its use.

Another difficulty with Web search engines is the quality of the results. In response to a search query, a search engine often lists irrelevant sources. Some of the best search engines will categorize results by, for example, the type of Web site such as commercial, educational, personal, and so on. This can be helpful, but it does not eliminate sites that are irrelevant. Sometimes, these can be eliminated only when a researcher goes to the sites and scrolls through them. Ordinarily, however, the first few hits are likely to be the most useful, and a researcher with experience can often avoid others that are inappropriate.

To get the best result, a researcher must know the features of each search engine and how to focus queries to take advantage of those features most effectively. A capable researcher will also keep abreast of changes to the search engines. Each engine includes tips at its site for searching with it. Also, with practice comes proficiency.

There are two basic kinds of searches: keyword and concept. A keyword search generates Web sources that use the exact terms that the researcher types. A concept search adds sources that use related words. In general, it can be said that the best results are obtained in a search for Web pages that contain very specific terms.

META SEARCH ENGINES

Meta search engines (sometimes called metacrawlers) run searches on more than one search engine simultaneously. They are the best tools for searching the most Web space possible. (It should be noted that nothing searches the entire Web, however.) Meta search engines include EZ2Find (**www.ez2www.com/**), Copernic (**www.copernic.com**, which requires a free downloadable program), Mamma (**www.mamma.com**), Metacrawler (**www.metacrawler.com**), Dogpile (**www.dogpile.com**), Profusion (**www.profusion.com**), and Kartoo (**www.kartoo.com**). A useful category-based search engine is Invisible (**www.invisible-web.net**).

CONDUCTING ONLINE RESEARCH

Considering the variety of information online, it is almost certain that you will find something related to any research you undertake. The ease and speed with which you can do this research is the unique aspect of the Internet.

PLAN AHEAD: ANALYZE THE FACTS AND IDENTIFY THE ISSUES

With research, the key to obtaining successful results is knowing where to start. Knowing where to start requires knowledge of the research sources available and of the tools that can be used to access those sources. To be most efficient, plan your research steps before going online.

The first step is to know what it is you are seeking. To avoid wasting time, state your objectives clearly and be sure that you understand the goals. To narrow the scope of your research, you may need to know the reason for the research or how the results will be used.

The second step is to determine which sources are most likely to lead you to the desired results. One way to gain a sense of where you want to look is to use a guide book (see, for example, the most recent edition of *The Internet for Dummies*, 9th Edition, which is written by John R. Levine and published by IDG Books Worldwide, Inc.). A good guide can point you in the direction of the right Web sites to visit to begin your research, to narrow its focus, or to find exactly what you need. Once these steps are taken, the research can begin.

With any source, you need to balance its utility and convenience against its credibility.

ONLINE RESEARCH STRATEGY

On the Internet, a researcher uses traditional and innovative approaches to research. For example, the use of a search engine is usually the first step in online research. It may be the last resort, however, if posting to a newsgroup (an online bulletin board service) would get a more reliable response from a primary source with less effort on your part than other methods. (Newsgroups are discussed in more detail later.)

STARTING POINTS

Sometimes, a research session begins with one of the online directories or guides discussed earlier in this chapter. For example, if the object of your search is to find a law firm that practices in a specialized area of the law, you could start with Yahoo's "Government" menu (**www.yahoo.com/Law**). This is broken into submenus including one titled "Law Firms and Legal Services." Within the list, there is a general list of "Firms" which can be arranged alphabetically.

A search engine or a meta search engine (such as **www.refdesk.com**) may be used to compile your own list of Web sites that contain certain key words. A search engine tailored to zero in on specific topical sites may be more useful than either a general search engine or a meta search engine, depending on your research goals. (Search engines geared specifically to legal resources are discussed later.) Keep in mind the limitations of search engines, however.

Your search may locate many irrelevant sources and may not spot every site that you would find helpful. In addition, different search engines will yield different results. For this reason, it is best to conduct a search by accessing more than one search engine.

From the preliminary results of a general search, you can click on the links to visit the sites and determine which are useful. Many sites include their own links to other sources that you may find helpful. Some Web sites attempt to collect links to all online resources about particular topics. These include directories, which were discussed earlier, as well as other sites such as The Federal Web Locator (**www.infoctr.edu/fwl/**), which provides links to federal offices and agencies. For more experienced online legal researchers, there is Hieros Gamos (**www.hg.org/index.html**), which is an extensive guide to legal information that is available online. Some sites are more eclectic in what they offer (see, for example, the 'Lectric Law Library at **www.lectlaw.com**).

CREATIVE SEARCHING

Information can be collected easily via the Internet. The only limit to what is collected and how it is analyzed is the ability of the researcher. What distinguishes a good researcher from an average researcher is the ability to get hard-to-find or obscure data from hard-to-reach sources that are especially reliable. Backing up a secondary source with hard-to-find primary data is the foundation of qualitative, comprehensive research.

For example, the Web can be a good source for obtaining background information on people. Imagine that a lawyer is scheduled to question a certain witness. Background information could be useful during the questioning. The witness's past can be investigated on the Web in several ways. A general search can be made to uncover any data that concern the witness. Newsgroups (discussed later in this chapter) can be searched to discover whether the person has said anything in the groups that relates to his or her testimony. Other ways to find people and information about them are discussed later in this chapter.

Interpreting the data in clever ways is another attribute that distinguishes good researchers from average researchers. Assume that, for example, one of your competitors advertises employment opportunities for engineers with certain skills. To a clever researcher, this may indicate a new direction for the competitor's research and development, or a new product line. A competitor's Web links could give you insight to the competitor's operations or indicate a new market for your products. To discover sites that link to your competitor's home page, you could use a feature such as the Advanced Search tool at the AltaVista search engine site (**www.altavista.com/**. In that tool, in the box that says Search with … this Boolean expression use **link:your competitor's home page address**. Thus, you simply type in the URL of your competitor's home page after the "**link:**".

DISCOVERING WHAT RESOURCES ARE AVAILABLE

Despite your best intentions and attempts to pinpoint your research, you may have to approach a project without a clear objective as to what it is that you need to find. Your initial research goal may be to discover the extent of resources available online, with your ultimate goal being to obtain more precise results.

Similar to the popular guides and directories such as Excite (**www.excite.com**), less familiar Web pages contain links to important resources in particular topic areas. These pages often include directory-style menus and search utilities. For example, legal resource search engines, such as CataLaw (see **www.catalaw.com**), are directed to find sites related to legal topics. Remember that these sources often change, and may even disappear, and that new ones can develop overnight.

Many libraries provide access to their catalogs online so that you can determine the availability of particular resources offline (see, for example, the cataloging available on the Web site of the New York Public Library at **catnyp.nypl.org/**). You can search these catalogs over the Internet in the same way that you would search them in the library. This can save the time that a futile trip to the library might cost. You can search the catalogs of your local libraries and those of libraries that are more distant. This allows a researcher to find source material at a distant library that might be delivered to a closer library where the researcher could more conveniently review it. You can also find and view covers of books that pertain to your search by use the A9 search engine found at **www.amazon.com** .

Another way to find what resources are available is to begin with a listserv list or a newsgroup. These can also be used to update your research.

A **listserv list** (or mailing list) is a list of e-mail addresses of persons who are interested in a particular topic. By placing their names on the list, they agree to receive e-mail from others about the topic. A message sent to the list's address is automatically sent to everyone on the list. Anyone on the list can respond to whoever sent the message. As a researcher, you might post a message that asks for suggestions as to online resources for your research. You can also add your name to the list to receive the mass e-mailings. In some cases, you may be able to browse an archive of messages to see if another researcher has previously called attention to a resource that matches your search. Listserv lists (see **www.tile.net/lists/**) provide more anonymity than newsgroups.

A **newsgroup** (also known as a **Usenet group**) is a forum that resembles a community bulletin board. A newsgroup can be selected by topic. A researcher can post a question or problem (for example, "Does anyone know a good source for what I want to know?") and check back hours or days later for others' responses. A researcher might also browse the newsgroup's archive, although messages are typically stored only for limited periods. There are thousands of newsgroups (a few hundred focus on law-related topics). Newsgroup directories can be skimmed at such sites as Liszt (**www.liszt.com/**). Newsgroups can be searched with specialized search engines such as Newsville at **www.newsville.com/news/groups/**.

USING BLOGS FOR LEGAL RESEARCH AND MORE

Millions of people generate blogs on a regular basis, and millions more will be doing so in the future. Blog is short for Weblog. In the legal field, try the links regularly provided by **www.inter-alia.net/**. If you click on "Current Issue," you may find links to up-to-day stories on legal issues, improvements and refinements for standard search engines, and more. To view more legal blogs, type those two words into any search engine.

NARROWING YOUR FOCUS

Once you find a Web site that could be useful, you may need to zero in more precisely within that site on specific data.

Many sites contain links to text and graphics within their pages. These links can be browsed to peruse documents within the site. Some sites include internal search engines with which you can look for specific information within those sites. These internal search engines are similar to an index in a book, except of course you choose the words in the index. Each site's internal search engine can be different, but in general, it will work like any search engine. (See, for example, Harvard University's internal search tool at **http://search.harvard.edu:8765/** allows you to search an extensive database of over 900 sites.)

Remember your browser also has the ability to search an individual Web page that you are viewing. This can be particularly helpful when scrolling through a document for a bit of information would be tedious and time-consuming. Using your browser's "find" tool, you can search, for example, the text of a specific bill before Congress at the Library of Congress's THOMAS site (**http://thomas.loc.gov**), which contains legislative information. You might also use your find tool to search a company's document in the Electronic Data Gathering, Analysis, and Retrieval (EDGAR) database of the Securities and Exchange Commission (SEC) (**www.sec.gov/edgar.shtml**). EDGAR is an indexed collection of documents and forms that public companies and others are required to file with the SEC.

EVALUATING WHAT YOU FIND

After you have found what appears to be exactly what you are looking for, you need to consider its reliability. In evaluating data revealed through a search on the Internet, a researcher applies the same evaluative skills he or she would use to evaluate data found in other, more traditional ways. Because anyone with access to a computer can put anything on the Internet, however, every online source of data needs to be specially considered for its credibility.

Is the source of the information a primary, a secondary, or a tertiary source? Primary sources include experts and persons with firsthand knowledge. For example, the inventor of a product would be a primary source for information about his or her invention. Publicly filed documents are also good primary sources. For example, the legal forms that some companies are required to file with the Securities and Exchange Commission are good primary sources for the information that they contain. Secondary sources include books and periodicals (such as newspapers and magazines), and their online equivalents that contain "secondhand" information. Tertiary sources are any other sources that might be used in research.

A researcher needs to be aware of how old data are and of other factors that could influence its validity. Is the information outdated? Is the source reputable? A reputable source might be an organization that has established itself as an excellent resource in a particular field. A less reputable source might be an individual's own self-serving home page. Was the information placed on the Web by a source that may be biased in a certain way?

In other words, a researcher needs to keep in mind that people can provide information on the Web whether or not they know what they are talking about. People may not even be who they represent themselves to be. When possible, it is best for researchers to find and interpret primary sources for themselves before forming conclusions.

GENERAL LEGAL RESOURCES

www.findlaw.com As pointed out before, FindLaw, which is part of West Group, is one of the most comprehensive sources of free legal information. You can access all federal and state cases, codes, and agency regulations, as well as journal articles, newsletters, and links to other useful sites and discussion groups.

www.ncf.edu/novak/vl/Alist.html   This extensive list of legal resources is arranged alphabetically. It bills itself as "Legal Resources without Charge."

www.law.cornell.edu   As we mentioned, the Legal Information Institute (LII) at Cornell Law School also is a great site for legal research and includes federal, state, and international law. You can access materials by topic or by jurisdiction, or you can browse through one of its topical libraries.

www.lectlaw.com/bus.html The 'Lectric Law Library has general legal resources as well as a "Business Law Lounge" for businesspersons.

www.hg.org/index.html Hieros Gamos offers legal and business resources from the United States and abroad.

www.lawguru.com/ilawlib The Internet Law Library provides many legal resources relating to American and foreign law.

www.washlaw.com/ WashLaw Web, sponsored by Washburn University School of Law, offers many links to legal resources on the Web.

www.law.com/index.shtml This site provides up-to-date legal news articles and information, and has links to other legal news publications, including the *National Law Journal*.

LEGAL RESEARCH IN CRIMINAL LAW

Sometimes you may be asked to do research in criminal law, particularly now that many businesses as well as businesspersons are being subject to criminal proceedings. Of course there are many good Web sites that deal with criminal law. Here is a listing of those that may help you the most:

jurist.law.pitt.edu/sg_crim.htm   Jurist's criminal law site, sponsored by the University of Pittsburgh School of Law, provides links to a wide variety of criminal law sources and topics, including news and legislation updates, important criminal law journal articles, and a "Best of the Web" section.

wings.buffalo.edu/law/bclc The Buffalo Criminal Law Center aims to "reinvigorate the study of criminal law" and its Web site promotes this goal by offering access to some of the most innovative criminal law research on the Internet. Students should pay particular attention to the "Penal Law: A Web" link, which leads to an exhaustive database of American criminal law.

www.abanet.org/crimjust/home.html Given the important role that attorneys play in the field of criminal law, it is not surprising that the American Bar Association (ABA) maintains a page dedicated to the topic. The site provides information on new studies supported by the ABA, as well as a database of relevant publications and court cases.

www.law.nyu.edu/library/foreign intl/criminal.html The amount of information on international criminal law on the Internet can be overwhelming, but this site, sponsored by the New York University School of Law, does a good job of identifying the subject's most important issues.

HELPFUL GOVERNMENT SITES

http://firstgov.gov The U.S. government's official Web site provides links to every branch of the federal government, including federal agencies.

www.loc.gov The Library of Congress has links to state and federal government resources, and the THOMAS system allows you to search through several legislative databases.

www.gpoaccess.gov/index.html The U.S. Government Printing Office posts official information from each of the three branches of the federal government, including publications such as the *Code of Federal Regulations* and the *Federal Register*.

www.uspto.gov The U.S. Patent and Trademark Office has a searchable database of patents and trademarks. This site also provides general information and a way to check the status of pending applications.

www.copyright.gov The U.S. Copyright Office provides information on copyrights and a searchable database of copyright records.

www.eeoc.gov/index.html The Equal Employment Opportunity Commission (EEOC) posts information on employment discrimination, EEOC regulations, compliance, and enforcement.

www.epa.gov The Environmental Protection Agency (EPA) offers information on environmental laws, regulations, and compliance assistance.

www.sbaonline.sba.gov The U.S. Small Business Administration assists in forming, financing, and operating small businesses.

www.usdoj.gov   The U.S. Department of Justice provides information on many areas of law, including civil rights, employment discrimination, crime, and immigration.

www.csg.org The Council of State Governments offers state news, information, legislation, and links to state home pages.

FEDERAL AND STATE COURTS

www.supremecourtus.gov The United States Supreme Court provides its case opinions, orders, and other information about the Court, including its history, procedures, schedule, and transcripts of oral arguments.

www.oyez.org/oyez/frontpage This site offers a multimedia guide to the United States Supreme Court, including a virtual tour of the building, and digital audio of oral arguments and Court decisions in cases.

www.uscourts.gov/index.html   The Federal Judiciary provides access to every federal court (including district courts, appellate courts, and bankruptcy courts).

www.ncsconline.org   The National Center for State Courts offers links to the Web pages of all state courts.

www.abiworld.org   The American Bankruptcy Institute is a good resource for bankruptcy court opinions, news, and other information.

UNIFORM LAWS

www.nccusl.org   The National Conference of Commissioners on Uniform State Laws (NCCUSL) posts the text of uniform laws (such as the Uniform Commercial Code) and information on state adoptions and pending state legislation.

www.law.upenn.edu/bll/ulc/ulc_frame.htm The University of Pennsylvania Law School, in conjunction with the NCCUSL, provides an archive of all drafts of uniform state laws.

CONSTITUTIONAL RIGHTS AND LIBERTIES

www.aclu.org The American Civil Liberties Union provides information on pertinent legal issues, such as privacy and discrimination.

FINDING PEOPLE

Public records are helpful in looking for people, but some records (including most historic records) are not on the Internet. Despite this limitation, Web searches can be cheaper and faster than going to a government office or a library.

BROAD SEARCHES

On the Web, a researcher can run a broad search with a general search engine such as Yahoo (**www.yahoo.com**). A researcher might also narrow the focus of a search to, for example, all of the U.S. phone books. There are several phone book Web sites. Each of the sites has its unique features. Some provide e-mail addresses (for example, Yahoo People Search at **http://people.yahoo.com**). Some include business listings (see, for example, BigBook at **www.superpages.com**). Some can conduct a search with a phone number or an e-mail address to reveal a name and a street address (see, for example, the Internet Address Finder at **www.iaf.net/**). On some sites such as WhoWhere (**www.whowhere.com/**), a search can be based on personal characteristics, such as occupation, school, or affiliation with a certain organization. Another phone book can also be searched at World Pages (**www.worldpages.com**).

NARROW SEARCHES

If something is known about a person, the Web can be a good source for locating him or her. For example, if you are looking for an attorney, you can link to West Legal Directory, which is a comprehensive compilation of lawyers in the United States, from **www.FindLaw.com.** On the front of the home page, use

"Find Lawyers!" Then you will have use of a search engine powered by West Legal Directory.

To look for a professor at a particular university or an employee at a certain company, the staff directory of the school or business firm may be available, and searchable, online. (See, for example, the directory for the faculty of the Harvard Law School at **www.law.harvard.edu/faculty/** .

INVESTIGATING COMPANIES

It is important to remember that sites on the Web can be searched online anonymously (without the awareness of the firm about which information is sought). Because of this anonymity, you may learn of competitive threats and opportunities without alerting your competitors.

FINDING COMPANY NAMES AND ADDRESSES

A researcher can run a search with a phone number to find a company's name and address (for example, see Verizon Superpages at **www.superpages.com**). Without a phone number, a company's name and address can be found with the help of a directory that searches by industry and state (see the Switchboard.com page at **www.switchboard.com,** for example). A search with such a directory can also help to determine whether a specific firm name is in use anywhere in the United States. You can find out about who owns a domain name by using the free services of Network Solutions, now owned by Verisign (**www.networksolutions.com**). On the top right of its home page, click on WHOIS.

UNCOVERING DETAILED INFORMATION ABOUT PUBLIC COMPANIES

To discover more information than a company name and address, an in-depth search is necessary. A guide to uncovering company information on the Web is located at **www.virtualchase.com/coinfo/index.htm**. You can follow a complete business research tutorial online to discover company information at **www.learnwebskills.com/company/index.html**. Most companies maintain their own Web sites, which may contain the firm's annual reports, press releases, and price lists. Some companies put their staff directories online.

Information may be available through the sites of government agencies. For example, the Occupational Safety and Health Administration (OSHA) site (**www.osha.gov**) identifies manufacturers whose products have caused injuries or deaths at any time in the last twelve years, and the Consumer Product Safety Commission (CPSC) site lists products that have been recalled (**www.cpsc.gov**). The Securities and Exchange Commission (SEC) regulates public companies and requires them to file documents and forms revealing certain information. The documents include annual reports and proxies, which contain information on directors and stock issues. This material can be accessed through the SEC's Electronic Data Gathering, Analysis, and Retrieval (EDGAR) online database at **www.sec.gov/edgar.shtml**.

Additional information about public companies can be found at other free sites as well as on pay sites. In general, the best free sites provide data on the companies and links to the companies' home pages, EDGAR, and other resources, such as news articles. See, for example, the Wall Street Research Network at **www.wsrn.com**. Pay sites sometimes include larger databases with archives of information that may span decades and may cover companies in other countries.

LEARNING ABOUT PRIVATE COMPANIES

Data on private companies is more difficult to find because these firms are not subject to the SEC's disclosure requirements. Much of the information that is available is only what the companies want to reveal. With this limitation in mind, a few sites compile some of the data on private companies, associations, and nonprofit organizations. For example, Hoover's Online at **www.hoovers.com/** provides brief profiles of many companies, with links to other sites, including search engines. For a fee, Hoover's will provide expanded profiles. Another source, which also gives lots of information on virtually all public companies, is at **www.corporateinformation.com/**

UPDATING THE RESULTS

Once you have determined that the results of your research are as current as possible given the limits of your source, you can confirm whether those results represent the most recent data available by going online. News sites abound on the Internet. There are general, consumer-oriented sites sponsored by such well-known news organizations as CNN (see **www.cnn.com**). There are sites directed at those who may be interested only in updates in specific subjects, such as the law (see, for example, FindLaw offers daily business and legal news services at **www.findlaw.com/**). Corporate press releases—both current and from archives—can be reviewed at PRNewswire's site (**www.prnewswire.com**). Other sources for updating research results include newsgroups (or Usenet groups) and listserv lists, both of which were discussed earlier in this chapter.

ADDITIONAL RESOURCE SITES ON THE INTERNET

As we have said, what is available on the Web changes rapidly. New sites come online. Old favorites disappear. Familiar sites move. URLs change. This section lists some additional sites that a legal professional might find helpful. Many of these sites are not otherwise noted here. Included are references to valuable sites that have been on the Web for some time and have been kept up-to-date. Note, however, that this list is not meant to be exhaustive.

BASIC RESOURCES

Important Web resources for a legal professional include more than law-related sites. As indicated earlier, other important sites can include those of your competitors. Sometimes, however, all that is needed is some basic information: the meaning of a word, the area code for a telephone number, or a local map, for example. Sites with such basic information include the following.

Almanacs and Nonlegal Encyclopedias. These may be found at a site maintained by Information Please at **www.infoplease.com**.

Case Citation Guide. An online version of *The Bluebook: A Uniform System of Citation*, which is compiled by the editors of law reviews at several distinguished law schools, is accessible at **www.law.cornell.edu/citation/**. (Click on various topics on the left.)

Dictionaries. A dictionary is provided at a site titled "WWWebster Dictionary" (Merriam-Webster, Inc.) at **www.m-w.com/netdict.htm**. Sites for legal dictionaries, multiple dictionaries, and specialized dictionaries are mentioned below.

E-mail Addresses. E-mail addresses may be located through the Internet @address.finder at **www.iaf.net/**.

Information about the Internet. Many sites that provide background information about the Internet. These include WhatIs?Com at **http://whatis.techtarget.com/** and the Internet Society (ISOC) at **www.isoc.org/**.

Internet Directories. A half dozen Internet directories, including Yahoo (**www.yahoo.com**) and Infoseek (**http://infoseek.go.com**) which were mentioned earlier in this chapter, are well known. Other Internet directories include "E-Map: The Electronic Map to the Internet" at **www.e-map.com/**. A site titled "Librarians' Index to the Internet" is at **http://lii.org**. Another useful directory is WebCrawler at **www.WebCrawler.com/**.

Internet Service Providers. To locate an Internet service provider, see the site ISP Finder at **www.ispfinder.com/**. Another source for the names of providers is the "Internet Access Providers Meta-List" at **www.herbison.com/herbison/ iap_meta_list.html**. The commercial service America Online can be accessed at **www.aol.com**.

Legal Dictionaries. There is a European law dictionary at **http://library.ukc.ac.uk/library/lawlinks/european.html**. The 'Lectric Law Library provides a dictionary of legal terms at **www.lectlaw.com/d-a.htm**. There is a "plain language" legal dictionary titled "WWLIA Legal Dictionary" at **www.duhaime.org/diction.htm** .

Library Catalogs. For lists of links to the catalogs of libraries that may be accessed online, consult Yahoo's Library Collection at **www.yahoo.com/Reference/ Libraries**. The Library of Congress offers a collection of links to other libraries' catalogs at **lcWeb.loc.gov/z3950/gateway.html**. For a list of the catalogs of law libraries that may be available, see Hieros Gamos' "Libraries and Library Catalogs" at **www.hg.org/toplibrary.html**.

Maps. U.S. Street Maps is a site that provides what its name implies at **http://maps.msn.com**. Another useful site is MapQuest at **www.mapquest.com/**. See also World Maps at **www.maps.com/**.

Multiple Dictionaries. On-Line Dictionaries includes links to more than 500 dictionaries in over 140 languages at **www.yourdictionary.com**.

Specialized Dictionaries. One Look at **www.onelook.com/** offers an engine that searches hundreds of dictionaries focused on such special topics as business, medicine, science, technology, and the Internet.

Telephone Directories. All U.S. phone books are online at Switchboard at **www.switchboard.com**. These books are also available at **www.555-1212.com**. A directory of toll-free numbers can be found at AT&T Toll-Free Solutions at **www.anywho.com/tf.html**

Thesauri. The WWWebster Dictionary site, produced by Merriam-Webster, Inc., includes a thesaurus at **www.m-w.com.** *Roget's Thesaurus* is accessible through a couple of URLs, including **www.bartleby.com/thesauri/.** Try also **www.thesaurus.com** .

Zip Codes. For zip codes, see the U.S. Postal Service site at **http://zip4.usps.com/zip4/welcome.jsp.**

UNIVERSITY SITES

Many universities, colleges, law schools, and other academic institutions are dedicated to making the Internet and its related technology an essential part of professional research. Their Web sites are often good points from which to start because in general they provide updated material and links to other resources. These sites include the following.

Law-related Starting Points. The Legal Information Institute at Cornell Law School is a good starting place for online legal research. The URL is **www.law.cornell.edu.** This site includes many United States Supreme Court decisions (within hours or days of their release) and links to many other law-related sites and services.

Another good site is the World Wide Web Virtual Law Library maintained by the Indiana University School of Law at **www.law.indiana.edu/v-lib/index.html.** This is a comprehensive, up-to-date, subject index of law-related topics.

LawLists, a site produced at the University of Chicago, is online at **www.lib.uchicago.edu/~llou/lawlists/info.html.** This site contains an extensive listing of law-related discussion groups, including legal listservs.

Meta-Index for Legal Research at Georgia State University College of Law (**http://gsulaw.gsu.edu/metaindex**) enables a researcher to run a search in several Web sites' internal search tools simultaneously.

Northwestern University, at Oyez Oyez Oyez: A Supreme Court Database (**www.oyez.org/oyez/frontpage**), provides digital audio (RealAudio) of the oral arguments in many important United States Supreme Court cases, as well as recordings of some of the announcements of the Court's opinions.

Law-related Discussion Groups. To receive information about new and updated resources related to the law, subscribe to LAWSRC-L by sending an e-mail note to **mailto:listserv@listserv.law.cornell.edu.** In the note, state, "subscribe LAWSRC-L <your name>".

ADDITIONAL GOVERNMENT SITES

The government—the federal government, in particular—provides many excellent resources online. Nearly every federal agency has its own Web site. Some of the most useful sites for a paralegal include the following.

Law-related Starting Points. The House of Representatives Library at www.house.gov is one of the best government-supported resources of material on the Web. This site contains the full text of pending legislation and congressional testimony. The "Law Library" section contains a wealth of legal resources. The Library of Congress's Thomas site (http://thomas.loc.gov) duplicates some of the House site's materials, but it does not include the "Law Library."

Business and Economic Information. The Web site of the U.S. Department of Commerce, at www.commerce.gov/, contains a wealth of business and economic statistical data and other information. Some of it is available only for a fee. There are links to other government agencies' sites, including the home page of the U.S. Patent and Trademark Office.

Government Publications. GPO Access is the title of the Government Printing Office's database containing the full text of the *Code of Federal Regulations*, the *Congressional Record*, the *Federal Register*, all versions of all bills introduced in Congress, the current *Government Manual*, the *United States Code*, and other government publications. The URL is www.gpoaccess.gov/databases.html.

Discussion Group. To learn about new government sources that appear on the Web, subscribe to GOVDOC-L. Send a message to mailto:listserv@ psuvm.psu.edu. The message should read "subscribe GOVDOC-L <your name>".

SITES FOR ASSOCIATIONS AND ORGANIZATIONS

Some online databases that catalog associations, professional organizations, and nonprofit organizations include the following.

Associations. Associations Online includes Web links to more than five hundred associations divided into categories. The address is www.ipl.org/ref/AON/ .

Yahoo's directory includes a list of professional associations at www.yahoo.com/Business and Economy/Organizations/Professional/.

Paralegal Organizations.   Directed specifically at paralegals is the National Federation of Paralegals Legal Resources site at **www.paralegals.org/displaycommon.cfm?an=1**.

Nonprofit Organizations. More than one million nonprofit organizations are included in a database maintained by the Internet Nonprofit Center at **www.nonprofits.org/**. This site includes links to the Web pages of many nonprofit organizations.

FREE COMMERCIAL SITES

Commercial sites are Web pages that are maintained or supported by for-profit organizations (as opposed to academic institutions, the government, and nonprofit organizations). Some commercial sites such as Westlaw® charge for their use. These are fee-based, or pay, commercial sites. Other sites pay for themselves with on-site advertising. These are free commercial sites. Free commercial sites that may be of value to a legal professional include the following.

All-purpose Starting Points. Yahoo organizes, categorizes, and subdivides the most comprehensive list of URLs on the Web. New Web addresses are added the rate of hundreds per day. Yahoo's address is **www.yahoo.com**.

   Internet orientation, Internet tools, and Internet guides are the subjects of the Internet Web Text Index at **www.december.com/ Web/text/index.html**.

   A collection of references to subject guides can be found at the Internet Public Library at **www.ipl.org** .

Law-related Starting Points. West Legal Studies Resource Center—is at **www.westbuslaw.com/**. This site includes daily law highlights, an overview of the U.S. court system, study aids for students, links to a law dictionary and a lawyers' directory, and more.

   "The Internet Legal Resource Guide" at **www.ilrg.com/** is an index of approximately four thousand law-related Web sites, categorized by topic. The site also includes the "LawRunner: A Legal Research Tool," which is preprogrammed to run your search terms in templates across as many as thirty million Web pages.

   The reference site called "Internet Tools for Lawyers" can be found at **www.netlawtools.com/research/index.html** . This site is both a guide to research on the Web and a good starting point with links to other online resources.

Law-related search engines are linked at "Virtual Legal Search Engines," a site produced by an organization called Virtual Search Engines, at **www.virtualfreesites.com/search.legal.html** . This site also includes a number of basic references (dictionaries, for example) and links to search engines for other topics.

"Law Library Resource Xchange" (LLRX) at **www.llrx.com/** provides links to a number of resource sites on the net, ranging from legal research to library products and services. This site, which is maintained by Law Library Resource Xchange, L.L.C., includes timely and updated articles relating to research and library topics.

Media Directory. The American Journalism Review site contains more than eight thousand links to the online pages of newspapers, magazines, and other media, at **www.newslink.org/menu.html**.

Appendix

Evaluating Online Resources

One of the major concerns that many people have about the Internet is also one of its main advantages. Anybody can (and many have!) put up their own information, or home pages on the Web, for everybody to see. Some of the same rules about evaluation of print material also apply to the Internet. This appendix reviews some of the points to consider when applying those rules to Internet resources.

Here are three basic tips to keep in mind. First of all, when you get to a Web site, find out who has created it. If it was created by an institution that you already trust, you can probably trust the information in its Web site. Second, ask yourself why the information is available to you. Commercial Web sites are on the Internet to sell products. Third, be aware that there are some groups who have found the Internet to be a really inexpensive and effective way to promote their point of view, even if it is off-the-wall, pornographic, or just plain wrong.

What Information Is Relevant?

Facts? Opinions? Statistics? Background information? What are you looking for? The first step in evaluating a source is to know exactly what information is relevant to your research. What is the purpose of your search? What is its focus? A good researcher tests resources against the purpose and focus of his or her search.

With a purpose and focus in mind, a researcher can refine his or her search. This is the key to finding information quickly. With only a vague notion of purpose and a couple of general search terms, a researcher will waste much time viewing irrelevant sources. By specifying two or more words that, for example, a Web page must contain, however, a researcher can narrow a search most usefully to links that are more on point. Other Web pages are noise. Most search engines will rank results according to how relevant they appear are to the terms used in the search. Some search engines will further help to refine a search. For instructions, click on their help links.

It is important at this point not to rely on only one search engine or site. The results of the same search conducted through different engines can vary, and it may take several searches before a researcher finds precisely what he or she needs. To discover more about the features of the various search services, go to **www.searchenginewatch.com**. At this commercial site, you can find basic information about how the engines work, and reviews and comparisons of their performance.

Who's Providing the Data?

When you first visit access a source on the Internet, scan it to determine who the author is and what organization is publishing or presenting the information. Some of the newest versions of some browsers can tell you who registered the Web site being viewed. There is also special software available that can supply this and other background information about Web sites.

Next, determine whether a source is primary or secondary. The Internet and the Web are rich in primary sources, but they also abound with secondary sources. The former allows a researcher to make his or her own interpretation and analysis. The latter consist of other persons' analyses. Be aware, that the Internet and the Web are also awash in sources with little or no credibility at all.

How Credible Is the Resource?

Once the source and the date of the data is known, the credibility of the source can be considered. Who specifically put together the resource? Who gathered the information and wrote the particular document? Is he or she qualified to write about the topic? Who is the publisher? Are the writer and the publisher authoritative, or at least reliable? Has the document been copyrighted? Who could be contacted for more information?

How Accurate Is the Information?

Although a source might be otherwise credible, the information that is provided may not be valid. An expert in any field is only as authoritative as he or she is up to date. The date checks are an important step in evaluating accuracy. In other words, are the data timely?

There are other, qualitative questions to ask. Is the presentation of the information without such errors as typographical mistakes, misspellings, and grammatical flaws? Is the presentation easy to follow? The answer to this question involves a look at a source's artistic display (its visual graphics) as well as it electronic organization (its links). Is the information organized so that it can be read easily? Are there charts and other illustrations to keep the presentation lively and the data understandable?

What about the information? Is it complete? Is it comprehensive and detailed enough for the purpose and focus of the research? Are the data concrete or is it vague? Is it plausible? Is it supported by authoritative references to other sources? In other words, is the source more than an opinion? This leads to another important question.

What about Objectivity?

Is the source suspect for any reason? Is it a spoof or a parody? Is it biased? If it is biased, in what ways does this bias show?

For the answers to those questions, consider the answers to these questions: Does the source of the information provide more than one side to an issue? Are the contentions of persons with other points of view acknowledged? Does the editorial tone appear to indicate that the presentation of the information is intended to persuade readers to adhere to a particular viewpoint or come to a certain conclusion? Is there advertising accompanying the content? Is the advertising related to the substance of the data? Does there appear to be a connection between the advertising and the tone of the editorial substance? There is software available that can reduce or eliminate the advertising that accompanies Web sites.

Are the Data Timely?

As another item to check, consider the timeliness of the data. Look for information about the date on which the information was first published. When was it last updated? In this regard, consider whether the work is still in progress, whether it is an ongoing project, and whether it has reached a final point. Are the references that the source credits also up to date? Was there a previous edition of the source? If so, is it acknowledged? Is it available so that it may be compared to the current edition?

For more on evaluating legal resources on the Web, see "The Virtual Chase: A Research Site of Legal Professionals," which can be found at **www.virtualchase.com/quality/index.html**. This site is supported by the law firm of Ballard, Spahr, Andrews & Ingersoll, LLP. Other materials on Internet research are provided at **www.aallnet.org/index.asp**, maintained by the American Association of Law Libraries.

The Internet and the Web offer new opportunities to enrich research. These opportunities have never been available before. The opportunities are in the wealth of the resources. It requires critical thinking skills to evaluate and use these resources effectively. Investing time and energy into learning and applying these skills can have quick and rewarding results. Becoming a critical evaluator of information and the sources of information is fundamental to the skills that researchers, and everyone else, are required to use their whole lives.